FESTIVE FOODS
INDIA

Sylvia Goulding

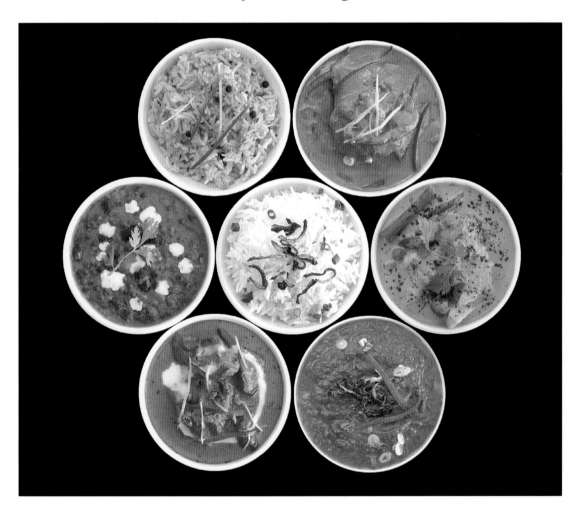

CHELSEA
CLUBHOUSE
An Imprint of Chelsea House Publishers

Chelsea Clubhouse
An imprint of Chelsea House Publishers
132 West 31st Street
New York, NY 10001

Library of Congress Cataloging-in-Publication Data

Goulding, Sylvia.
  Festive foods / Sylvia Goulding. – 1st ed.
    v. cm.
  Includes bibliographical references and index.
  Contents: [1] China – [2] France – [3] Germany – [4] India – [5] Italy – [6] Japan – [7] Mexico – [8] United States.
  ISBN 978-0-7910-9751-9 (v. 1) – ISBN 978-0-7910-9752-6 (v. 2) – ISBN 978-0-7910-9756-4 (v. 3) – ISBN 978-0-7910-9757-1 (v. 4) – ISBN 978-0-7910-9753-3 (v. 5) – ISBN 978-0-7910-9754-0 (v. 6) – ISBN 978-0-7910-9755-7 (v. 7) – ISBN 978-0-7910-9758-8 (v. 8)
  1. Cookery, International. 2. Gardening. 3. Manners and customs. I. Title.
  TX725.A1G56 2008
  641.59–dc22

                                    2007042722

Chelsea Clubhouse books are available at special discounts when purchased in bulk quantities for businesses, associations, institutions, or sales promotions. Please call our Special Sales Department in New York at (212) 967-8800 or (800) 322-8755.

You can find Chelsea Clubhouse
on the World Wide Web at
http://www.chelseahouse.com

Printed and bound in Dubai

10 9 8 7 6 5 4 3 2 1

For The Brown Reference Group plc:
Project Editor: Sylvia Goulding
Cooking Editor: Angelika Ilies
Contributors: Carey Denton, Jacqueline Fortey, Sylvia Goulding
Photographers: Klaus Arras, Emanuelle Morgan, Dirk Scholz
Cartographer: Darren Awuah
Art Editor: Paula Keogh
Illustrator: Jo Gracie
Picture Researcher: Mike Goulding
Managing Editor: Bridget Giles
Production Director: Alastair Gourlay
Editorial Director: Lindsey Lowe
Children's Publisher: Anne O'Daly

Photographic Credits:
Front Cover: Fotolia: Colinda McKie (inset); Klaus Arras (main)
Back Cover: Klaus Arras
Alamy: P. Kapoor 29, Mehdi Chebil 36; **Corbis:** Ric Ergenbright 18; **Fotolia:** Colinda McKie 34; **iStock:** title page, 6, 16, 31, 40; **Shutterstock:** 4, 5, 7, 8, 9, 10, 12, 13, 14, 20, 22, 23, 28, 29, 30, 32, 37, 38, 39

With thanks to models:
Anouk, Bundhalee, Caspar, Fidan, Hannah

Cooking Editor
Angelika Ilies has always been interested in cookery and other countries. She studied nutritional sciences in college. She has lived in the United States, England, and Germany. She has also traveled extensively and collected international recipes on her journeys. Angelika has written more than 70 cookbooks and cooking card series. She currently lives in Frankfurt, Germany, with her two children and has spent much time researching children's nutrition. Both children regularly cook with their mother.

Contents

let's START COOKING

Cooking is fun—you learn about different ingredients and cooking methods, you find out how things taste, and and you can serve a meal to your family and friends that you have cooked yourself! Some of the recipes in this book have steps that need adult help—ask a parent or other adult if they will be your kitchen assistant while you cook a meal.

This line tells you how many people the meal will feed.

In this box, you find out which ingredients you need for your meal.

WHAT YOU NEED:

SERVES 4 PEOPLE:

2¼ cups white rice
4 eggs, beaten
light soy sauce
4 tablespoons
   groundnut
   or soy oil
2 green onions
⅓ cup peeled shrimps
⅓ cup ham
⅓ cup green peas

Check before you start that you have everything you need. Get all the ingredients ready before you start cooking.

◁ When I grow up, I want to be a chef. Perhaps I'll even open up my own restaurant. And I'll be serving lots of delicious Indian meals—I like them best.

! WHEN TO GET help

Most cooking involves cutting ingredients and heating them in some way, whether frying, boiling, or cooking in the oven. Each time you see this exclamation mark, be extra careful as you cook and make sure your adult kitchen assistant is around to help.

For many meals you need to chop an onion. First cut off a thin slice at both ends. Pull off the peel. Cut the onion in half from end to end. Put one half with the cut side down on the chopping board. Hold it with one hand and cut end-to-end slices with the other hand. Hold the slices together and cut across the slices to make small cubes. Make sure you do not cut yourself!

Other recipes in this book use fresh chilies. Always wear rubber or surgical gloves when chopping chilies. If you don't have any gloves, wash your hands very thoroughly afterward, and do not touch your skin for a while. Chili seeds and the white pith contain a substance that makes your skin burn. Trim off the stalk and halve the chili lengthways. Scrape out the seeds and throw them away.

A **rolling pin** is a useful kitchen tool for rolling out the dough if you make Indian breads, such as chapatis, naans, rotis, or parathas.

Spice grinders are great for grinding seeds and spices, such as cumin seeds. You can also use a clean coffee grinder or mortar and pestle.

A **wok** is a Chinese skillet, but it is useful for cooking Indian dishes too. If you don't have a wok, you can use a heavy, deep skillet instead.

A **thali** is an Indian serving platter with little aluminum dishes. They are not essential, but look nice filled with different Indian snacks and rice.

A trip around
INDIA

India has many states. Its people speak different languages, observe different religions, and celebrate different festivals. They all enjoy delicious food.

India is the world's seventh largest country. It is about one-third the size of the United States. India is shaped roughly like a triangle. At the "top" is the snow-covered Himalayas mountain range. From there it stretches southward into the Indian Ocean, with the Arabian Sea in the west and the Bay of Bengal in the east. India shares borders with Pakistan in the northwest; with China, Bhutan, and Nepal in the north; with Myanmar in the east; and with Bangladesh in the east.

The capital is New Delhi. It is in the larger urban area called Delhi. Other important towns are Mumbai (Bombay), Kolkata (Calcutta), Chennai (Madras), Bangalore, and Hyderabad.

A variety of climates

India's climate is mainly tropical. This means that it is always fairly hot, and the winters are dry. There are four seasons: winter, summer, monsoon season in the southwest, and the after-the-monsoon season. The monsoon is a torrential rain that brings much-needed water for people and crops.

◁ **More than 1.1 billion people** live in India. That's one-sixth of all the people on Earth! Hindi is the official language of all India. Hinduism is India's main religion.

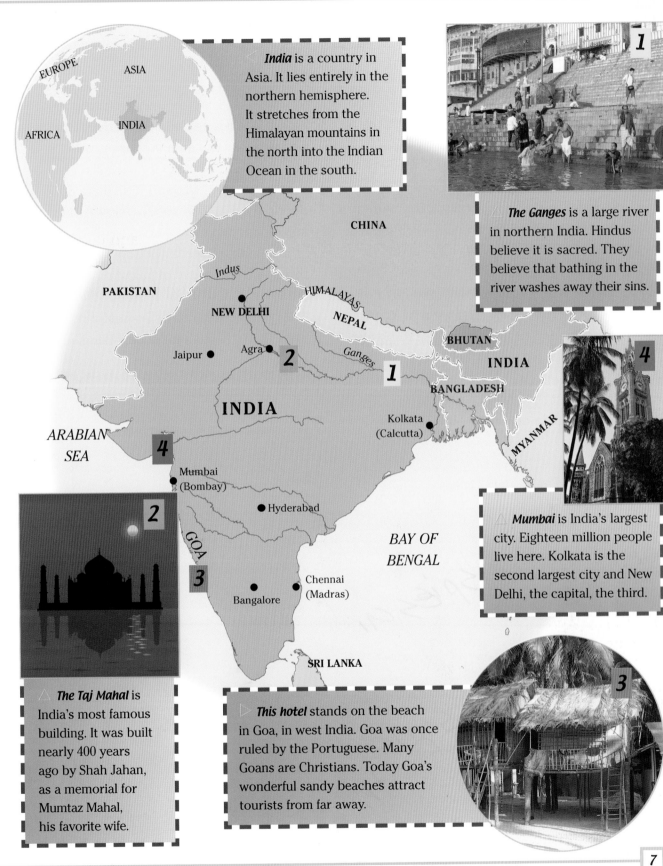

India is a country in Asia. It lies entirely in the northern hemisphere. It stretches from the Himalayan mountains in the north into the Indian Ocean in the south.

The Ganges is a large river in northern India. Hindus believe it is sacred. They believe that bathing in the river washes away their sins.

Mumbai is India's largest city. Eighteen million people live here. Kolkata is the second largest city and New Delhi, the capital, the third.

The Taj Mahal is India's most famous building. It was built nearly 400 years ago by Shah Jahan, as a memorial for Mumtaz Mahal, his favorite wife.

This hotel stands on the beach in Goa, in west India. Goa was once ruled by the Portuguese. Many Goans are Christians. Today Goa's wonderful sandy beaches attract tourists from far away.

Northern India

The great Himalayas stretch across several countries. A large part of the range lies in northern India. The third tallest mountain on Earth, Kanchenjunga (28,208 ft), is in the Indian Himalayas. Most of the peaks are covered in snow all year round. Many of India's major rivers start in these mountains: the Indus, the Ganges, and the Brahmaputra.

At the southwestern tip of north India is the state of Rajasthan, with the great city of Jaipur. In the southeast of north India is the state of Uttar Pradesh. Here is the town of Agra, with the Taj Mahal memorial. Between Rajasthan and Uttar Pradesh are the states of Haryana and Delhi, with the capital New Delhi.

The plains

Most of India's north, center, and east is a vast, fertile, and almost treeless plain. Millions of Indians live here and rely on the water of the great rivers from the Himalayas. There is also plenty of groundwater in the plains. This makes the land easy to water, and so much of India's food is grown on the plains.

The Ganges River flows eastward into the Bay of Bengal. Its delta (or mouth) covers a large area. The area is shared by India and Bangladesh. The vast city of Kolkata is located in this low-lying wetland. The delta often gets flooded, and it also suffers terrible hurricanes known as typhoons.

The Indus River flows from the Himalayas through the country of Pakistan. It then enters India and ends in the Arabian Sea. The course of the river Brahmaputra is from Tibet through India into Bangladesh.

▽ *This pleasant lake* is in Jammu and Kashmir, an area that is controlled by India. Other parts of Kashmir are controlled by Pakistan and China. Each of these three countries believes it should control the entire Kashmir region.

South India

South of the river plains lies the Deccan Plateau. Between this highland and the coasts are two mountain ranges. The Eastern Ghat mountain range is in the east and the Western Ghat mountain range is in the west.

This part of India has a tropical climate—it is always lush, green, and humid. Many wildlife reserves are in the South, and India's only rain forest is also here.

Musicians play traditional instruments in Rajasthan, a state in India's northwest. People make music and sing, dance, and tell poems. Folk songs tell of heroic deeds and love stories.

DO YOU SPEAK HINDI?

More than 1,000 different languages are spoken in India! Each state has its own official language. The official language of the Union of all Indian states is Hindi. Some important Indian state languages are: Assamese, Bengali, Gujarati, Hindi, Kannada, Kashmiri, Konkani, Malayalam, Marathi, Oriya, Punjabi, Sanskrit, Sindhi, Tamil, Telugu, Urdu. Many people also speak English.

The food we grow in
INDIA

Two-thirds of all people in India work on farms. India is one of the world's main food producers.

I n recent years, much more food has been grown in India than before. Farmers sow better seeds, and they use more fertilizers. They water the plants in dry times and drain the land during floods. This has helped crops to grow. India sells exotic fruits and vegetables, spices and tea to other countries.

Food staples

The northern Indian state of Punjab is one of the most fertile areas in the world. It is known as India's "bread-basket" because most of India's wheat grows here. People in northern India make flour from the wheat and bake many different kinds of bread, called chapati, naan, roti, or paratha. In southern India, the farmers grow more rice. Here people prefer rice instead of bread with their meals.

The northwestern state of Rajasthan borders Pakistan. Here most oilseeds are grown. Spices are mainly cultivated in the south, especially in the state of Kerala.

Tea and coffee are other important Indian products. Sugarcane and potatoes are also grown in many parts of India.

Keeping animals

In the countryside, many Indians keep cattle for milk. Many people do not own a tractor, and so they also use the cows to plow the fields. People who follow the Hindu religion do not slaughter cows and do not eat beef. But they do keep buffaloes. Buffaloes give milk and work the fields. When they are too old, they are slaughtered and eaten.

Legumes

People in India also grow many legumes—lentils, peas, and beans. These foods are good to grow for many reasons. Legumes contain many proteins. This makes them an ideal alternative to meat for India's many vegetarians. They are made into *dhals (see pages 16–17)*, and these are an important part of people's diets. Legumes are also an important fodder for cattle. And legumes are good for the soil in which they grow, too.

There are many different types of legumes. In India, the most important ones are green beans (mung beans), black matpe or urad beans, pigeon peas (arhar peas, tur peas), garbanzos (chickpeas), green peas, and all the different types of lentils.

▽ **Tea grows** in three main regions in India: Darjeeling tea grows in the foothills of the Himalayas; Assam, or breakfast tea, grows in the moist, fertile lowlands around the river Brahmaputra; and Nigiril tea flourishes in the hilly Blue Mountains in the South.

A CUP OF SPICE

Masala Chai is a popular tea—chai is the Indian word for "tea," and masala means "spice." To make the tea spicy, cloves, cinnamon, nutmeg, ginger, cardamom, or pepper is added to the tea leaves.

The spices

A wonderful variety of colorful and fragrant spices grows in India. Spices were once very valuable. The Portuguese, the Dutch, and the British took control of India centuries ago so they could get these spices for themselves.

Among the many aromatic spices grown in India are: ajwain, aniseed, cardamom, celery, chili, cinnamon, clove, coriander, cumin, dill seed, fennel, fenugreek, garlic, ginger, mustard, nutmeg, pomegranate seed, saffron, tejpat, turmeric, and vanilla.

Meals are cooked with many different spices and spice mixes. *Garam masala* is a typical spice mixture. It means "hot spices." But spices are not only used to flavor food. They also have medicinal properties—some aid digestion, others can help cure a cold, for example. Spices are also used to make cosmetics and soaps.

Competition has made life difficult for small spice farms. When other countries offer the same spice at a lower price, Indian farmers lose business. So some Indian farmers have started to grow new types of spices. They might start growing vanilla instead of chilies, for example, or they may grow organic spices.

Fish and seafood

India has long coastlines and many rivers. People have fished along India's coasts for thousands of years. Many only had small boats and no modern equipment, so their catch was low. Some fishermen have set up cooperatives to share expensive equipment.

India's most important fishing region is the southern state of Kerala. Inland rivers and lakes also have fresh fish, such as trout. And fish are also bred in fish farms. One of India's most important products is shrimps. These feature in many Indian dishes, for example in coconut pilao from Kerala.

Chili is one of seventy-five different spices that are grown in India. More spices come from India than from any other country in the world. After picking, the chilies have to be sorted, spread out to dry, and then packaged.

▽ *Fishermen sell their catch* in the city of Kochi, in southwestern India. Fish and seafood are sold in local markets. Families get there early to buy the freshest fish of the day. Kochi is an important fishing port.

SACRED COWS

In India, cows are everywhere. They wander the streets and do not worry about the traffic. This is because people who follow the Hindu religion believe that cows are sacred animals. So Hindus do not slaughter cows, and they do not eat beef or veal.

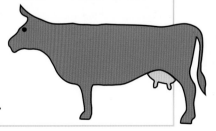

let's make...
GARAM MASALA

Garam means "hot," and *masala* means "spices." So this is a hot spice mixture! Every region and every family in India has its own special recipe for combining spices; here is one.

WHAT YOU NEED:

MAKES 1 SMALL JAR OF POWDER:

1 tablespoon cumin seeds
2 tablespoons coriander seeds
1 tablespoon cardamom pods
1 tablespoon peppercorns
1–2 dried chilies
2 cinnamon sticks
1 teaspoon cloves
1 bay leaf
½ teaspoon ground macis

◁ Traditional spice mixtures in India include twenty or more different spices. But even a basic mix will give your dishes a special Indian flavor.

HOW DO I USE <u>garam masala</u>?

Garam masala is a spice mixture. It is used for cooking savory Indian dishes. It can be used in two ways: it is either fried at the beginning of cooking a dish, or it is sprinkled in at the end.

1 Heat a dry skillet over medium heat without adding any fat. Add the cumin and coriander seeds, the cardamom, peppercorns, chilies, cinnamon sticks, and cloves.

2 Dry-roast the spices for a few minutes, stirring them with a spoon so they don't burn.

3 Allow the spices to cool a little, then crush them with a pestle in a mortar or grind them in a spice mill. Stir in the macis.

4 Put the spice mix into a container with a lid and keep it in a cool, dark place. It will last for several weeks.

To MAKE Sambar masala

In a dry skillet, dry-roast 10 tablespoons coriander seeds, 8–10 dried chilies, 1 teaspoon cumin seeds, 1 teaspoon black peppercorns, and 1 teaspoon fenugreek over medium heat for a few minutes. Put the roasted spices into a bowl. Now dry-roast 1 teaspoon each of split white beans, yellow mung beans, and yellow split peas for a few minutes, stirring so they won't burn. Add them to the spices. Turn off the heat. Grind or pound the spices and legumes as above. Warm 2 tablespoons ground turmeric in the still-warm skillet and stir into the powder.

let's make...
LENTIL DHAL

A *dhal* can be two things: legumes that have been shelled and split, or a stew made from the legumes. In southern India, many people are vegetarian. They particularly love dhals.

WHAT YOU NEED:

TO SERVE 4 PEOPLE:

10 ounces yellow split lentils
salt, black pepper
1 red and 1 green bell
  pepper
1 bunch green onions
3 garlic cloves
3 red chilies
2 tablespoons ghee or
  cooking oil
1 teaspoon each garam
  masala *(see pages
  14–15)*, turmeric,
  coriander seeds,
  and ground cumin

◁ We eat dhal every day, even for breakfast. We eat different ones each time. Some are sweet, most are savory. Some are quite thick, others are soupy. I serve dhal with bread and a bowl of plain yogurt.

WHAT'S THIS: dhal?

Dhal means "pea" or "lentil." In the West we call them legumes or pulses. There are more than seventy different types in India. They are hulled, which means their shell has been removed. And they are split. Try these in your cooking:
- chana dhal (split yellow garbanzos)
- masoor dhal (red lentils)
- mung dhal (mung beans)
- muth dhal (brown-green beans)
- rajma dhal (kidney beans)
- urad dhal (urad or black gram, a bit like black lentils)

1 Wash the lentils. Pick over them and throw away any that look a different color or empty.

2 Put the good lentils into a saucepan with 2½ cups cold water. Add ½ teaspoon salt and grind in lots of pepper. Bring to a boil. Cover the pan, reduce the heat to low, and cook gently for about 25 minutes. The lentils should be cooked but not too soft. !

4 Peel and finely chop the garlic. Trim, deseed, and chop the chilies (*see page 5*). !

5 Heat the ghee or cooking oil in a wide skillet. Add the pepper, green onion, garlic, and chilies. Fry and stir for about 2 minutes. !

6 Add the spices and fry for a few seconds. Add the lentils together with their juices. Stir and heat through. Season with salt and pepper and serve. !

3 Meanwhile, wash and trim the vegetables. Cut the bell peppers into thin strips and the green onions into thin rings.

let's make...
CHAPATIS

Breads are particularly popular in northern India, where most of the country's wheat is grown. We make lots of different breads: chapatis, parathas, naans, and rotis.

◁ An Indian girl mixes the flour to help her mother make chapatis. Chapatis are great for soaking up sauces and for scooping up rice and meat.

WHAT YOU NEED:

MAKES 12 CHAPATIS:

¾ lb atta or roti flour
1 tablespoon salt
1 tablespoon cooking oil
1 cup lukewarm water

WHAT'S THIS: *atta* OR *roti flour?*

Atta is an Asian flour. It is ground from very hard durum wheat grains. Roti is a flour made from millet. You can find both in Asian delicatessens, or use wholegrain wheat flour instead.

1 Stir together the flour and the salt. Add the oil and the water. Knead to make a smooth dough. Allow the dough to rest at room temperature for at least 2 hours.

2 Divide the dough into 12 portions. Shape each portion into a ball. On the floured work surface, roll out each ball to make a circle of about 4 inches.

4 Heat a cast-iron skillet without oil. One at a time, put the dough circles into the skillet. Cook them for a few seconds on both sides until they puff up and start showing small brown spots.

3 Thinly dust the dough circles with flour so they don't stick together. Pile them all on top of each other.

5 Once cooked, put all the chapatis into a basket and wrap them in a cloth to keep them warm.

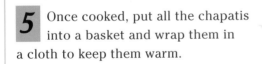

How we celebrate in
INDIA

India is a land of many festivals: every occasion is celebrated with great spectacles, special food, and rituals.

*T*here are festivals to mark the different seasons or the arrival of the full moon. Religious festivals honor India's many gods and goddesses, or they remember an important mythological event. National festivals celebrate the founding of modern India. Some holidays are celebrated all over the country, but they have different names in different states. People also eat different festive foods to celebrate.

Independence Day

All Indians celebrate the creation of modern India. On August 15, people remember the day India gained independence from Great Britain in 1947. They raise the Indian flag in schools and offices and sing the national anthem. Friends and families get together and share lunch or dinner. There are also many kite-flying competitions around the country.

Another national holiday is Gandhi Jayanti on October 2. It honors Mahatma Gandhi, the great political and spiritual leader of the nonviolent movement for independence from Britain. Gandhi inspired many others. He is known as the "Father of the Indian Nation."

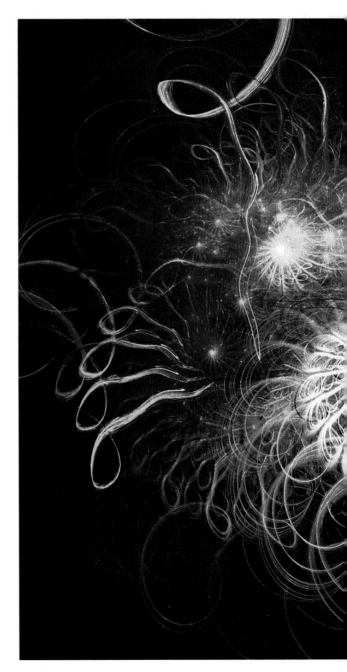

Diwali – The Festival of Lights

Diwali is properly called Deepavali. The festival was originally celebrated by followers of the Hindu, Sikh, and Jain religions. But the celebrations are so enjoyable that people of other faiths also celebrate Diwali.

There are many different stories about the origins of Diwali. One of the most widely believed stories tells of the battle between Rama and Ravana. Lord Rama is a Hindu god. His enemy, Ravana, had kidnapped Rama's wife. But in the battle Lord Rama won. Diwali remembers his victory. At the same time, it is the victory of good over evil. It also marks the victory of light over darkness.

Diwali is celebrated over five days in October or November each year. To celebrate the triumph of light, people light clay lamps called *dipa* or *deeya*. They also set off amazing fireworks all over India. People clean their homes, feast together, have fun fairs, and give each other gifts. Special Diwali candies are made or bought for the day. *Barfi* are made from condensed milk and sugar, and *badam barfi* are made with rosewater and almonds.

Diwali fireworks are lit in every area neighborhood. There are spinning fire circles called *zameen chakra* and huge fire mountains called *anaar*. Lots of noisy fire crackers and rockets are lit in every street.

BRIGHT LIGHTS

On one of the days of the Diwali festival, many lamps are lit. The lamps make each home look bright, and the streets are also festively lit. Light symbolizes knowledge. Lighting many lamps celebrates an end to ignorance.

Ramzan Id

Muslims are the second largest religious group in India. The most important Muslim celebration in India comes at the end of the month of Ramzan. (Ramzan is often known as Ramadan elsewhere.) During Ramzan people follow a strict fast for a whole month—they do not eat or drink anything during the day. But they may eat and drink at night, between sundown and sunrise. Often, people share the first meal after the daily fast with family and friends. This meal is known as *iftaar*.

At the end of the month of fasting there are great celebrations, called Ramzan Id or Ramzan Eid or Id-ul-Fitr. Muslims pray together and give alms (gifts) to the poor. People dress up, visit family and friends, and go to fairs. Children often get *eidee*—special

△ **This statue** in New Delhi shows the Hindu god Lord Shiva. Each religious group in India has its own gods and goddesses, and their great deeds are celebrated.

△ **For the Holi Festival**, this girl has had plenty of colored powders thrown at her. Women and men often wear white clothes so the colors show up well. They dance and sing and hug and wish each other "Happy Holi."

holiday money to buy toys and trinkets. The favorite Ramzan Id snack is *seviyan*, a sweet vermicelli dessert with nuts and raisins.

The Holi Festival

Holi, or the festival of colors, is another Hindu festival that has become popular with other faiths. It marks the end of winter and the arrival of spring. People celebrate the new, green growth of leaves and the colorful flowers and blossom of the trees.

To celebrate these spring colors, people throw colored powders and water at each other. Everyone tries to look as colorful as possible. Old people join in as much as the young. The powders were originally made from natural herbs. As well as providing decoration, they were meant to protect people from spring flu and colds. Today the powders are made from artificial colors.

GLITTERY CANDIES

Festival candies are sometimes made to look extra special with an edible silver or gold leaf.

let's make...
VEGETABLE CURRY

For festivals such as Diwali we usually eat vegetarian food. We use as many different vegetables as possible to make a curry—this is symbolic for having plentiful food all year round.

WHAT YOU NEED:

SERVES 4 PEOPLE:

⅔ cup dried blackeye beans, soaked in water overnight
1 onion
2 garlic cloves
1-inch piece fresh ginger
1½ lbs vegetables (as many different types as possible, for example baby corn cobs, carrots, okra, green onions, tomatoes)

3 tablespoons cooking oil
1–2 tablespoons garam masala
about 1¼ cups hot water
salt, black pepper
2 tablespoons fresh cilantro leaves

◁ This is a satisfying meal and delicious too. Serve it with rice or some Indian breads to soak up the sauce.

WHAT'S THIS: <u>blackeye beans?</u>

Blackeye beans are also known as cowpeas. They are a good food for vegetarians because they contain lots of protein. When they are soaked and cooked, the beans swell—1 cup of dried beans makes about 2½ cups of cooked beans.

1 Drain the beans. Put them into a saucepan and cover with cold water. Bring to a boil. Drain in a sieve and refresh the beans under cold running water.

2 Return the beans to the saucepan and cover with water. Bring to a boil again. Reduce the heat, cover, and simmer over low heat for about 50 minutes until the beans are almost soft. Check from time to time and add more water if the beans are no longer covered with water.

3 Meanwhile, peel the onion, garlic, and ginger. Finely chop the onion and the ginger. Crush the garlic. Wash and trim the other vegetables. Cut all the vegetables into bite-sized pieces.

4 Heat the oil in a deep, wide saucepan. Add onion, garlic, and ginger and fry for a few minutes, until they are a golden yellow.

5 Add the vegetables, a few at a time, starting with the hardest. Fry and stir for 2 minutes, then add more and fry and stir. Sprinkle the garam masala on top and fry for another minute. Pour in the hot water and stir.

6 Drain the beans and add them to the vegetables. Stir, cover, and simmer over low heat for 15 minutes. Season with salt and pepper. Sprinkle with cilantro leaves and serve.

let's make...
SEVIYAN

After a month of fasting in Ramzan, people look forward to the big feast at the end, the Eid-ul-Fitr. The highlight is seviyan, a sweet milk and vermicelli noodle dessert.

WHAT YOU NEED:

MAKES 6-8 PORTIONS:

- 1 teaspoon green cardamom pods
- 1 tablespoon ghee or cooking oil
- 4 ounces seviyan (thin vermicelli noodles from India or Pakistan)
- 7 cups milk
- 2 tablespoons raisins
- 1 tablespoon chopped almonds
- 1 tablespoon finely chopped pistachio nuts
- ½ cup sugar
- ⅛ cup cream

◁ Muslim men often give each other seviyan or other sweet dishes as a Ramzan gift. People even call the festival "sweet Eid" because of this dish.

WHAT'S THIS: ghee?

Ghee is a clarified butter—it contains no particles or water. To make ghee, butter is simmered until all the water is gone. You can usually find ghee in the ethnic section of your superstore. You may use cooking oil as a substitute.

1 Break open the cardamom pods. Ease out all the seeds and chop them with a large knife.

2 Heat the ghee or cooking oil in a saucepan. Add the cardamom seeds and fry them for a few seconds. In a separate pan, heat the milk (make sure it doesn't boil over!).

3 Break the noodles into smaller pieces. Add them to the pan with the ghee and the spices. Over medium heat, fry them lightly for a few minutes, or until they are a light brown color.

4 Pour in the hot milk. Bring to a boil. Reduce the heat and simmer for about 5 minutes, stirring all the time, so it doesn't burn.

5 Stir in the raisins, almonds, and pistachios. Allow everything to simmer for about 15 minutes, until the mixture has thickened a little. Stir often so it doesn't stick to the bottom.

6 Take the saucepan off the heat. Stir the sugar and the cream into the mixture. Decorate. Serve hot or cold—the seviyan thickens as it cools.

How we celebrate at home in
INDIA

Family ties are very important in India. All celebrations are held with the entire family. People visit their relations and they share a festive meal. Often they give each other gifts of candies and nuts.

Birthdays

Like children all over the world, children in India enjoy celebrating their birthdays. Hindu children often get a new outfit to wear on this special day. If their birthday is on a school day, they take candies into school to hand out to their classmates. At home they enjoy a delicious meal with their family, maybe a curry dish. It is followed by the special birthday dessert, *dudh pakh*, a spiced rice pudding with nuts and fruit.

A birthday cake is also a must in India, and so are gifts and sometimes a party. Family and friends will visit or telephone to "wish you," which means "happy birthday." Muslim children may also celebrate their birthday with a cake and candles, but many

The bhindi or red dots on this girl's head count as festive marks in southern India. Drops and sparkling gems have also become fashionable. In the rest of the country, it is mainly married women who wear a *bhindi*.

Muslim families do not celebrate birthdays. They save their celebrating for the special festival of Ramzan Eid.

Children's Day is an international festival. In India it is celebrated on November 14, on the birthday of India's first prime minister, Jawaharlal Nehru. Nehru was often called *Chacha* (Uncle) Nehru by children. Some families hold a children's party on that day.

Rakhi

Rakhi is the celebration of the love between brothers and sisters. In India this also includes stepbrothers and stepsisters, and cousins. It may even be celebrated by close family friends who are not related.

If the brother and sister can get together, there is a big ceremony. The sister paints a *tilak (see the box below)* on the brother's forehead. Then she ties on his *rakhi*, or thread bracelet. In return, the brother makes a solemn promise that he will always protect his sister. The brother's gift to his sister may simply be his blessing. But he may also give her some candies or other gift, for example some jewelry, new clothes, or money.

△ **This boy has his rakhi** tied on by his mother rather than his sister. He now gives his sister a promise. For as long as he lives he will make sure that his sister is not in danger and that she is well looked after.

FACE-PAINTING

A tilak is a decoration on a man's forehead. It shows that he belongs to the Hindu faith. The decoration may be a horizontal or vertical line, or more than one lines, a U shape, or a dot. The paint is made from red sandalwood paste, ashes, clay, or turmeric powder.

After this, the sister performs *aarti*. This is a Hindu prayer that people sing on special occasions. She carries a tray holding an oil lamp, flowers, and food around her brother. Then she offers him some candies.

Food is important at rakhi. Samosas *(see pages 34–35)* are often eaten at family parties. Candies are a traditional rakhi gift. *Ladoos* are particularly popular. These are round candies flavored with nuts and spices.

Life-cycle celebrations

Hindus mark the different stages of a person's life with rituals that are called *samskara*. There are sixteen different samskara celebrated

△ **These schoolchildren** are at Amber Fort in Rajasthan. Once they finish their education, they will have a big party. The end of school life is a *samskara,* or a life stage, in a Hindu's life. After this stage, people are thought to be ready to get married.

during a person's life. Some mark the arrival of a new baby or when it is named. One is celebrated when a boy's hair is cut for the first time after birth.

On the first day of school, many Hindus pray to Saraswati, the Goddess of Learning. In southern India, the children celebrate the day by eating a sweet rice porridge, with raisins and nuts, called *sarkarai pongal.*

Weddings

A marriage is an important day in anyone's life. In India, it is also a life-cycle celebration or *samskara*. At a wedding, people believe, it is not only the bride and groom who are brought together, but their families as well. The celebrations can last five or seven days. The guests eat plenty of festive food together, so they can get to know each other.

Traditional weddings start with a *mehndi*, or henna party, the night before the wedding, at the bride's home. Instead of jewelry, the bride has lacy or flower patterns painted on her hands and feet. After the wedding, the bride does not have to do any work until the *mehndi* has washed off.

▽ *Mehndi* is a henna paste that is used to make patterns on the skin. It is safe and natural. The tattoos last from a few days to a month. A mixture of lemon juice and sugar is brushed onto the henna to make it set.

let's make...
TANDOORI CHICKEN

For special family celebrations, people eat this traditional chicken dish. They cook it over charcoal in a clay oven called a *tandoor* and from which the dish gets its name.

WHAT YOU NEED:

SERVES 4 PEOPLE:

2 garlic cloves
2-inch piece fresh ginger
juice of 1 lemon
4 teaspoons tandoori
    spice mix
½ cup low-fat yogurt

4 chicken legs
2 whole chicken
    breasts with bones
cooking oil for
    brushing
salt

PLUS:

2 onions, cut into rings
2 teaspoons ground cumin
a little lemon juice,
    diluted with water
lemon wedges and fresh
    cilantro leaves
    to garnish

 Tandoori chicken is my favorite! You can try tandoori lamb or tandoori shrimps, too, using the same method.

WHAT'S THIS: tandoori spice mix?

Tandoori spice mix combines many spices—cardamom, cinnamon, cloves, coriander, cumin, ginger, nutmeg, paprika, pepper, salt, and turmeric. Red paprika and yellow turmeric make the mixture orange in color. Some store-bought mixes include food coloring.

1 Peel and finely chop the garlic and ginger and put them into a bowl. Add the spices and yogurt, and stir well to combine. **!**

2 Wash the chicken legs and breasts under running cold water, then pat them dry with paper towels, and put them into a bowl. Rub or brush with the yogurt mix. Cover the bowl and chill in the fridge for at least 12 hours.

3 Preheat the oven to 450°F. Take the chicken pieces out of the yogurt sauce, and pat them dry with paper towels. Place them on a rack and roast in the oven for 20 minutes.

4 Turn the chicken pieces over, brush them with a little oil, and sprinkle with salt. Cook for another 20 minutes in the oven. **!**

5 Place the cooked chicken pieces on a platter. Scatter the onion rings and cumin over the top, and drizzle with lemon juice. Garnish with lemon wedges and cilantro.

SAFETY WITH chicken

• Make sure you rinse and pat dry the raw chicken with paper towels.
• Wash cutting boards and knives in hot water after using.
• Scrub your hands thoroughly before and after handling.
• Never ever put raw chicken and cooked chicken on the same plates or cutting boards.

let's make...
SAMOSAS

Samosas are a great snack food. They can be made with lots of different fillings. We eat them with a spicy dip or chutney— my brother always has the hottest chili sauce with it!

WHAT YOU NEED:

MAKES 16 TO 20 SAMOSAS:

3½ tablespoons ghee or oil
2 cups flour

1 teaspoon salt
1 teaspoon lemon juice

FOR THE FILLING:

2 tablespoons ghee or oil
7 ounces potatoes
1 small zucchini
¼ cauliflower
2 teaspoons garam masala

1 teaspoon ground ginger
½ teaspoon turmeric
1 teaspoon Cayenne pepper
½ teaspoon ground cumin salt

PLUS:

ghee or cooking oil
for frying

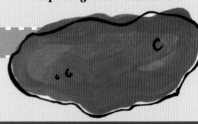

◁ For dipping, I serve a store-bought sweet chili jam with my samosas.

WHAT SORT OF _fillings_ ARE THERE FOR SAMOSAS?

North Indian or Punjabi samosas are large and plump. They often have a potato-and-pea filling with raisins or cashew nuts. Gujarati samosas are tiny and filled with lots of different vegetables. In Hyderabad, people add a spoonful of yogurt to the samosa dough.

1 Melt the ghee and mix it with the flour, ½ cup lukewarm water, salt, and lemon juice. Knead for about 10 minutes to make a smooth dough. Wrap the dough in plastic wrap and allow to rest for 30 minutes.

2 Make the filling. Peel and cube the potatoes. Wash, trim, and cube zucchini and cauliflower. Heat the ghee in a small saucepan. Add the vegetables. Fry and stir for 2 minutes. Add the spices and fry and stir for 1 minute. Add ½ cup water and cover the saucepan. Turn heat to low and simmer for 10 minutes. Remove the lid and simmer until all the liquid is gone. Allow to cool.

3 Knead the dough again, then roll it out thinly in small portions. Place a saucer (7–8 inches in diameter) on top of the dough. Cut out a dough circle around the saucer. Knead the leftover dough pieces, roll them out again, and cut more circles.

4 Cut each circle in half. Put 1 heaped teaspoon of filling in the center of each half-circle. Moisten the edges with water. Fold one corner on top of the other (see above). Gently squeeze the straight and the round edges together.

5 Heat the ghee or oil in a skillet. Fry the samosas, a few at a time, for 2 minutes. Carefully turn them over and fry for 2 more minutes. Lift them out with a slotted spoon and drain on kitchen paper.

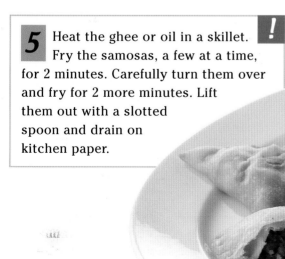

How we live in
INDIA

India is a country of vast contrasts. It has huge sprawling cities and tiny villages. It invents the very latest in technology. But some people still live in very traditional ways. India has international airports, and bullocks pull carts through the busy city streets. There are some very rich and many very poor people.

City life

Many young people leave the villages to find work in the cities. Some cities have brand-new offices. Here people make new computer programs and systems. Some Indians work in call centers or science centers for companies in other countries. They have well-paid jobs and live in brand-new apartments. But many others live in poverty. Their houses are made from scrap materials. And thousands of Indians have to beg and sleep on the streets.

The Cyber Gateway is a futuristic office building in Hyderabad in eastern India. A whole area is called HITEC city. Companies that make new computer and science products are based here.

An Indian woman in a village sells traditional handicrafts. Indians produce beautiful silk and cotton clothes, colorful rugs and carpets, and attractive silver and fashion jewelry.

Village life

The majority of Indian people live in small villages. Many villages now have electricity, and some have piped water. In other villages, the people dry cow dung to use as fuel for cooking. Women get water from a well and carry it home in buckets on their heads. They wash their clothes at a nearby river or stream.

Many people in the villages belong to a cooperative. They share tools and machines. They may work together at a dairy farm or

at a leather factory, or grow trees, or make cellphones, for example. They all share the work and the money they make.

For entertainment, the people who own a TV set may invite their neighbors to watch with them. People also get together to chat.

School life

Children go to school from 9 A.M. until 1 P.M., older children until 3 P.M. Most take a packed lunch—often rice, chapatis, and vegetables. In the villages, school may be in the open air or in one room with an earth floor. In the cities there are good state and private schools.

All children in India have to go to school between the ages of six and fourteen. But many cannot afford to go to school if the

△ **Street vendors** sell vegetables straight from their farm. Popular varieties are okra, tomatoes, potatoes, eggplant, bitter gourds, carrots, and onions. Many Indians are vegetarians, and vegetables are cheap.

journey is too far away to travel to every day. Children often need to look after younger brothers and sisters. Many children have to help their families or earn money.

Family life

It is common for several generations to live together in India. Grandparents, uncles and aunts, and cousins may all live together in the same house. When a man gets married, his wife comes to live in his family's house. But in the cities the space is cramped. Often it is not possible for so many people to live together.

Mealtimes are family time. A *thali* is a common meal in India. It is named after the silver tray it is served on. Different sections of the tray hold rice, chapatis, chutney, and a curry such as a vegetable curry or *rogan josh. Dhal* is another popular dish. This stew is made with spiced lentils or beans. It is an important dish for vegetarians because it has plenty of protein. Indians enjoy a cooling yogurt drink called *lassi* or fresh fruit juices.

▽ **Indian Railways** runs one of the largest and busiest railroad networks in the world. It is also the largest employer in the world—more than one million people work on the trains.

Time off

Going to the movies is the most popular way to spend spare time in India. The so-called "Bollywood" films mix adventure and love stories with song and dance. People also enjoy reading the gossip about their favorite movie stars. Cricket is the top favorite sport in India. The country has many professional cricket teams, and people play cricket whenever they get a chance.

BOLLYWOOD

More movies are made in India than anywhere else in the world. The movie industry is called "Bollywood"–it takes the letter "B" from Bombay, the former name of Mumbai, and the rest from Hollywood.

let's make...
LOVELY LASSI

This is a super chilled yogurt drink! It's refreshing on hot days, and in winter I just leave out the crushed ice. Lassi also helps cool your mouth if you are eating a very spicy dish.

▽ I just love drinking lassi!

WHAT YOU NEED:

MAKES 6-8 GLASSES:

4 cups yogurt (at least 3.5% fat)
1 cup chilled water
salt
½ teaspoon ground cumin
1 teaspoon lemon juice
crushed ice
some fresh mint leaves

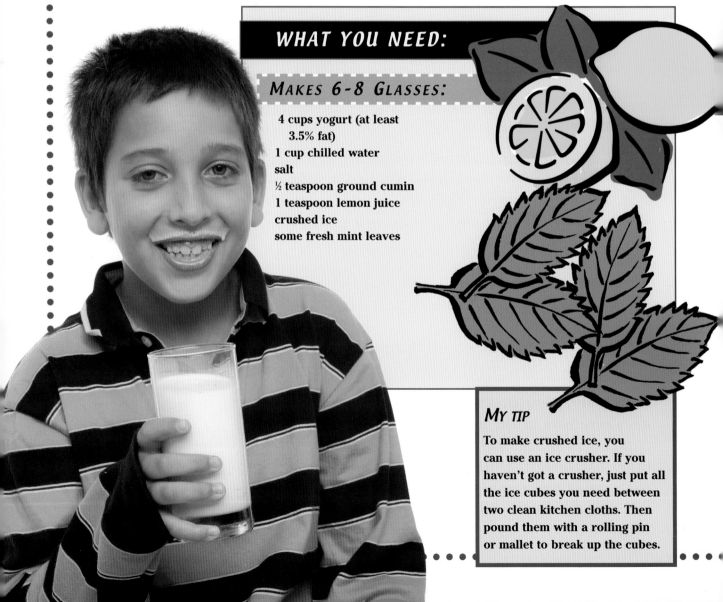

MY TIP

To make crushed ice, you can use an ice crusher. If you haven't got a crusher, just put all the ice cubes you need between two clean kitchen cloths. Then pound them with a rolling pin or mallet to break up the cubes.

1 Put the yogurt, chilled water, salt, ground cumin, and lemon juice into a bowl or measuring cup. Using a spoon or a whisk, stir all the ingredients thoroughly to combine them well into a smooth mixture.

2 Half-fill the glasses with crushed ice *(see My Tip opposite)*. Pour the lassi on top of the ice. Decorate with fresh mint leaves. Cheers!

SWEET VARIATION: Mango Lassi

In a blender, purée the flesh of 1 mango together with 4 cups full-fat yogurt, 1 cup chilled water, and 4 tablespoons sugar. Put crushed ice into glasses and pour the mango lassi on top.

let's make...
ROGAN JOSH

This dish was originally cooked with mutton and plenty of aromatic spices. It is a classic North Indian family favorite, and every family has their own recipe.

WHAT YOU NEED:

SERVES 4 PEOPLE:

2 lbs lamb (from the leg)
½-inch piece ginger
3 garlic cloves
2 onions

5 tablespoons ghee
½ cup yogurt (10% fat)
salt
fresh cilantro leaves

FOR THE SPICE MIXTURE:

½ teaspoon ground
  cardamom
a pinch of ground
  cloves
½ teaspoon ground
  black pepper
a pinch of ground
  cinnamon

1 teaspoon hot paprika
1 teaspoon ground
  coriander
1 teaspoon ground
  cumin

◁ Serve the
rogan josh with
boiled rice or with
chapatis *(see pages 18–19).*

WHAT'S THIS: <u>mutton?</u>

Mutton is an older sheep; lambs are very young sheep. Mutton meat has a stronger flavor, but it can be tough. It is ideally cooked for a long time as a stew.

MY TIP

If you can get hold of it, why not try cooking this dish with goat meat instead?

1 Wash the lamb under cold water and pat it dry with paper towels. Cut the meat into bite-sized chunks.

2 Peel and finely chop the ginger, garlic, and onions. Combine all the spices in a small bowl.

3 Heat the ghee or oil in a large saucepan. Add the meat chunks and fry them all over, stirring, until they no longer look pink.

4 Take out the meat and set it aside. Add the ginger, garlic, and onions. Fry for 2 minutes. Add the spice mixture, stir, and fry for 2 minutes.

5 Return the meat to the saucepan. Add the yogurt, 1 cup water, and 1 teaspoon salt and stir. Simmer everything over low heat for 1 hour.

6 Stir the curry from time to time. Add more water if it gets too dry. Garnish with fresh cilantro and serve with boiled basmati rice.

let's make...
COCONUT PILAU

This recipe is an everyday dish from the southern state of Kerala. Many dishes there are vegetarian, but seafood is also popular. Coconut is a typical local ingredient.

WHAT YOU NEED:

SERVES 4 PEOPLE:

2 cups basmati rice
salt
2-inch piece fresh ginger
1–2 chilies
4 garlic cloves
2 teaspoons ground cumin
1 teaspoon ground
   cardamoms
a pinch of ground cinnamon
1 large onion
3 tomatoes
2 tablespoons cooking oil
½ cup yogurt (10% fat)
½ cup unsweetened
   coconut milk

¾ lb peeled
   cooked shrimps
   (or firm fish fillet
   or cubed chicken)
2 tablespoons
   cashew nuts,
   chopped and
   roasted
a handful of green
   onion rings

◁ I like shrimps, and the bigger, the better. They're easy to shell—just pull off the head and the tail, pry the shrimp open at the belly, and pull off the shell. Yummy!

WHAT'S THIS: pilau?

Pilau is originally an Arabic word. There are many different spellings and pronunciations: pilaf, pilav, pilao. The main ingredients are usually chicken or seafood. Often, coconut, nuts, or dried fruits are added to the dish. It always has many spices.

1 Wash the rice in a sieve. Put it in a saucepan, add 2½ cups cold water and 1 teaspoon salt. Bring to a boil, stir, and cover. Simmer over low heat for 15–20 minutes. Add a little more water if it looks dry. **!**

2 Meanwhile peel the ginger and garlic. Trim and deseed the chilies (see page 5). Put ginger, garlic, chilies, cumin, cardamom, and cinnamon into a cup with 3 tablespoons water. Purée with a handheld blender or in the mixer until it is a fairly smooth paste.

3 Peel and chop the onions. Chop the tomatoes. Heat the oil in a deep skillet. Add the onion and fry it until it is golden brown. **!**

4 Add the spice paste and stir well. Stir in the tomatoes, yogurt, and coconut milk. Cook over medium heat for 10 minutes, stirring from time to time. Stir in the shrimps and cook for 3–4 minutes.

5 Stir in the rice and season with a little salt. Scatter the roasted cashew nuts and onion rings over the top of the dish and serve.

Look it up
INDIA

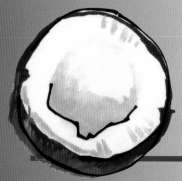

chapati one of many different types of bread in India

chutney a dipping sauce

dhal (1) a legume, a dried split bean or pea; (2) a stewlike dish made from legumes

Diwali the Hindu Festival of Light, one of the greatest Indian celebrations

garam masala a spice mix, literally "hot spices;" it is often sprinkled over a dish at the end of cooking

ghee clarified butter; you can use cooking oil instead

henna a plant material used for making temporary tattoos

Holi a festival that involves throwing color and paint over each other

mehndi (1) a temporary henna tattoo, applied to hands and feet, especially before a wedding; (2) the party, when wedding tattoos are applied

lassi a popular yogurt drink

legumes also known as pulses, shelled and split beans or peas commonly used in Indian cooking

samosa a deep-fried pastry triangle filled with vegetables or meat

samskara a life-cycle celebration, such as birth, name-giving, first day at school, or a wedding

seviyan a sweet dessert dish, eaten or given for the Muslim festival Ramzan Eid

tandoor a clay oven; it develops great heat and is used for cooking meat dishes like tandoori chicken as well as breads

tandoori spice mix a reddish/yellowish spice mixture used to marinate chicken or other dishes before cooking in the tandoor oven

thali a silver tray used to hold several different Indian dishes or chutneys

Find out more
INDIA

Books to read

Engfer, Lee. **India in Pictures** (Visual Geography). Lerner Publications: 2002.

Heydlauff, Lisa, and Upadyhe, Nitin. **Going to School in India**. Charlesbridge Publishing: 2005.

Kalman, Bobbie. **India: The Culture. The Land. The People.** Crabtree Publishing: 2000/2001.

Landau, Elaine. **India.** Children's Press, CT: 2000.

Swan, Erin Pembrey. **India** (Enchantment of the World. Second Series). Children's Press, CT: 2002.

Web sites to check out

http://india.gov.in
The official Indian government site

http://india.gov.in/knowindia/kids.php
The Indian government's Kids Corner, providing information on history, culture, and national symbols

www.historyforkids.org/learn/india/ food/index.htm
Information on Indian food and history, especially for children

www.kidswebindia.com
Aimed at kids and young teens, with information on India and its regions, festivals, recipes, news, puzzles, gardening advice, and much more

www.pitara.com
News, puzzles, and fun relating to India, for children

Index
INDIA